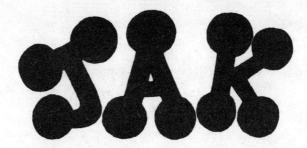

CARTOONS No. 26

from

Evening Standard

and

The Mail

ON SUNDAY

ORION

Orion Books
A Division of the Orion Publishing Group Ltd
Orion House
5 Upper St Martin's Lane
London WC2H 9EA

First published by Orion 1994

ISBN 1 85797 953 4

Printed and bound in Great Britain by
The Guernsey Press Co. Ltd, Guernsey, Channel Islands

**Wednesday
6 October 1993**

Sylvester Stallone, star of the violent Rambo and Rocky movies, tried to throw off his image as a muscle-bound bimbo by appearing nude on the cover of style magazine Vanity Fair, as Rodin's classical statue, The Thinker.

"I know what's different, Arthur! Sylvester hasn't got any socks on!"

Thursday 7 October 1993

It was revealed that Transport Minister Steven Norris had been enjoying an extraordinary number of adulterous affairs – much to the chagrin of the respective mistresses, each of whom believed themselves to be the only woman in his life.

**Friday
8 October 1993**

Viscount Linley, one of Britain's most eligible bachelors, son of Princess Margaret and nephew of the Queen, married Serena Stanhope, 23-year-old daughter of Viscount Petersham. He is a furniture maker.

"Lord Linley made all the chairs!"

**Wednesday
13 October 1993**

An administrator at
Ealing NHS Trust
Hospital said that up to
16 patients a night had
been sleeping in corridors
since April because the
council's social services
department was taking
up to two months to find
places in nursing homes.
The hospital was forced
to reopen 12 of the 75
surgical and medical
beds that had been closed
because of a shortage of
money.

"Think yourself lucky. Some people can't even get a bed!"

Vivienne Westwood showed her triumphant spring 1994 collection in Paris and supermodel Kate Moss drew the short straw and came out in only a strip of striped blazer fabric, barely covering her bottom.

"First, how much did it cost? Second, where's the rest of it?"

**Thursday
21 October 1993**

Austen Donnellan was cleared by an Old Bailey jury of raping another student after a drunken Christmas party. But the case highlighted the strange justice of the trial. The unsubstantiated charge of rape forced Mr Donnellan to undergo a traumatic trial, while his accuser was legally entitled to retain her anonymity and recover in obscurity.

"An intimate candle-lit dinner for two, certainly. With or without lawyers?"

**Friday
29 October 1993**

Woman bodybuilder Kimberley-Anne became one of the most talked about women in Britain because of her appearance in a billboard car advertisement. "She is built like a VW Vento," said the ad.

"I'm afraid it desperately needs a perm!"

Police and government declared an uneasy truce as Home Secretary Michael Howard retreated from the full-scale reform package proposed four months earlier by businessman Sir Patrick Sheehy. The idea of fixed-term contracts for every police officer was abandoned and Mr Howard decided not to interfere with traditional pension rights.

"Well, for a start, Sir Patrick, wasting police time! And we'll think of a few more on the way to the station!"

Princess Diana was photographed by a hidden camera as she exercised in a gym. Fitness club boss Bryce Taylor took the Peeping Tom pictures of Diana as she used a muscle-toning machine and sold them to the Mirror newspaper group. Bosses at the newspaper were branded as seedy little men in the widest condemnation ever of a newspaper by Buckingham Palace, politicians, editors and the public.

"Could you hold it like that for a minute while we change the film?"

Merseyside vicar Clive Kirke refused to baptise a baby Damien because he claimed the name is associated with the devil. New mum Gaynor Brennan was asked to choose another name "like John" rather than that of the child in the film The Omen. Gaynor had her baby baptised a week later at another church. He was named . . . Damien. The name derives from the 4th century Cilician Saint Damian who became patron saint of doctors.

"Is Damien a family name, then?"

**Wednesday
17 November 1993**

DIY enthusiast Peter
Ellis was jailed for
18 years for attempted
murder after trying to
electrocute his wife in the
bath. He plotted to kill
Lisa Ellis, 32, so he could
get £616,000 insurance
and move in with his
mistress, who for four
years had had no clue
that her lover was still
living with his wife.

"Roger! Have you been wiring up the bath again?"

England's footballers went out of the World Cup and manager Graham Taylor said he would stand down. England scored the seven goals needed against San Marino but, more absurdly, allowed the opponents the luxury of the third goal in their international history after nine seconds. Holland's sterling 3-1 victory in Poland made the result academic anyway.

"Imagine you wake up and find you're Graham Taylor? I am Graham Taylor!"

**Tuesday
23 November 1993**

Jeremy Paxman and
David Dimbleby took
part in an extraordinary
showdown to decide who
would take over the
BBC's Question Time
chair. Earlier in the
month incisive
interviewer Paxman had
been blackballed by The
Garrick Club by at least
four anonymous
committee members.

"One last question, Mr er . . er . . Paxwell. What clubs do you belong to?"

London Underground faced claims for more than £1 million after power failure hit both the morning and evening rush hours. More than 20,000 passengers had to be led through freezing tunnels from stranded trains in the biggest mass evacuation in Tube history when a power failure immobilised large parts of the network.

"I'm not sure, but I think we change onto the Northern Line at the next station!"

Camilla and Andrew Parker Bowles have a marriage of convenience, Andrew Parker Bowles's sister-in-law Carolyn claimed. "Ever since they married, they have had a fairly free life together. Which suits them both," she explained. Mrs Parker Bowles's statement confirmed what "everyone" knew, but her remarks on the Parker Bowles's menage highlighted how some "open" marriages seemingly work well.

"Actually, Tarquin, your mother and I have had a marriage of convenience for so long I'm not terribly sure which one she is!"

Former tycoon Roger Levitt walked free from court after he was sentenced to 180 hours of community service following his conviction on a charge arising from the collapse of his £150 million financial empire.

"I want Roger Levitt's lawyer!"

Eton College appointed a New Zealander as headmaster. John Lewis, of Geelong Grammar School in Australia and a rugby enthusiast, was named to succeed Dr Eric Anderson.

"They're not being unfriendly, Colonel, just practising the Haka for the new head!"

LILLEY'S NHS BENEFITS TEST

STAGE 3

25 Yds

KEEP CLEAR

DO NOT FEED

JAK

Social Security secretary
Peter Lilley announced
plans for a stringent new
medical test to be applied
to people claiming benefit
because they are unable
to work.

"... now we come to agility – this is worth 25 points!"

Close friends of the Princess of Wales disclosed that she intended to distance herself further from the Royal Family by leaving Kensington Palace and moving to a new home with her children. She had described the London residence as "secure, but a gilded cage".

"Desirable area! Look, I'm not really allowed to say, but guess who's just acquired two floors above the fish shop!"

Britain's record-buyers took the fat and spotty Mr Blobby to their hearts and snapped up 200,000 copies of his record, taking it to No 1 in the charts.

"You mark my words, it's only a matter of time before they put him up for the Garrick!"

Thursday 9 December 1993

The Archdeacon of York, the Venerable George Austin, publicly questioned whether Prince Charles could be trusted with the role of King. He said on BBC radio he believed the affair with Camilla Parker Bowles has shown him capable of breaking his word. "Charles made solemn vows before God in church about his marriage, and it seems he began to break them almost immediately. How can he go into church, into Westminster Abbey, and take the Coronation vows?"

"The way things are headed with the Church, it looks as if I'll have my Coronation in a registry office!"

The Prince of Wales was locked in battle with bishops over his moral suitability to be King. Senior Church figures voiced misgivings over his relationship with Camilla Parker Bowles. The criticism of Charles, led by the Archdeacon of York, the Venerable George Austin, threatened a major split in the Church of England.

"Ello! Ello! Who got rid of this troublesome archdeacon then?"

A poll of the Anglican
Synod showed that
nearly half of them felt
Prince Charles should
not become head of the
Church if rumours of his
adultery with Mrs
Camilla Parker Bowles
were proved.

"The vicar had just thrown the first stone at Prince Charles, when the stained-glass window fell on him!"

**Thursday
16 December 1993**

Tory MP David Faber split up from his wife, TV weather girl Sally Faber. The press made much of her having had horseriding lessons from Princess Diana's admirer Major James Hewitt. The attractive blonde, who keeps two horses at her farmhouse home on Dartmoor, reportedly enlisted Major Hewitt's help "to develop her skills as a one-day eventer".

"Lock up the weather girls, here comes the galloping major!"

London's internationally renowned orchestras – the Philharmonia, the London Philharmonic and the Royal Philharmonic – emerged battered but intact after six months of agonising over their future. The Arts Council, initially set on funding only one of them in future years, bowed to public pressure and agreed to continue funding all three at roughly the same levels as before.

"Well it took a year to come to a no-change solution, but we did have some damned good lunches!"

It emerged that Prince Edward had fallen in love with 28-year-old attractive blonde, Sophie Rhys-Jones. They had known each other for three months. But Royal aides were swift to caution against speculation of an imminent engagement. Meanwhile, Mr Blobby fever raged throughout Britain.

"Very well, Edward, but you'd better let me tell your father who's going to be best man!"

"Albert Roux? My husband's bought an ostrich by mistake. How long do I cook it in the oven, and at what gas mark?"

Wednesday 29 December 1993

A British woman of 59 gave birth to twins on Christmas Day. The babies were born by caesarian section in a London hospital. Their mother became the world's oldest to give birth to twins. They were born thanks to the pioneering work of Italian fertility expert Dr Severino Antinori.

"What a lot of weight you've put on, darling! Or are you being treated by that awful Italian doctor?"

Premier John Major gave 70 awards to ordinary folk picked by the public in the New Year's Honours. He removed the traditional glitz and glamour from the honours, with only a few awards going to celebrities, and cut the number of awards to civil servants by 60.

"I don't know if it's escaped your attention Henry, but you're the only one without a gong!"

**Tuesday
4 January 1994**

Two of the world's top bra firms shaped up for the mother of all battles in a market worth an estimated £20 million a year in Britain alone. Lingerie giants Playtex and Gossard declared war after Playtex grabbed the rights to Wonderbra which had been made by its archrival under licence for 30 years.

"With a cleavage like that, do you think he's wearing a Wonderbra or an Ultrabra?"

Rail and Tube passengers were hammered by huge fare rises of up to six times the rate of inflation. Hundreds of thousands of passengers were confronted with big increases in the cost of travel as they bought BR, bus and Tube tickets.

"I've decided to have my salary paid directly to British Rail and live on what's left over!"

Royal Mail announced it would be using a set of Prince Charles's watercolours to adorn a new set of stamps. The five stamps were made to commemorate the 25th anniversary of Charles's investiture as Prince of Wales.

"An utterly ravishing block of 25p stamps by Prince Charles. What do you think, Brian?"

Former Government Minister Tim Yeo confessed to fathering another illegitimate child. Just days after resigning his post over the love child he shares with Tory councillor Julia Stent, the MP admitted he had a 26-year-old daughter who was adopted at birth. Meanwhile, strict rules banning couples from choosing the colour of test-tube babies were demanded after news from Italy that a black woman had given birth to a white baby. The 37-year-old African, married to a white man, wanted a white woman's eggs to ensure her child did not suffer racism.

"We never told you before Cynthia, but you were a designer baby. However,
the technique was in its infancy then!"

John Major confronted a Tory Party in turmoil, a Cabinet split over moral values, and a country bemused by his back-to-basics policy theme. With his Ministers and MPs reeling from the shock of headline-making scandals and resignations, he needed to restore the credibility of a regime battered by the Tim Yeo affair, the controversies surrounding Tory MPs Alan Duncan, David Ashby, and Steven Norris, along with the tragic events surrounding the Earl of Caithness.

"Robin, I want you to go out there and get some woman into trouble. People are beginning to think of us as the boring party!"

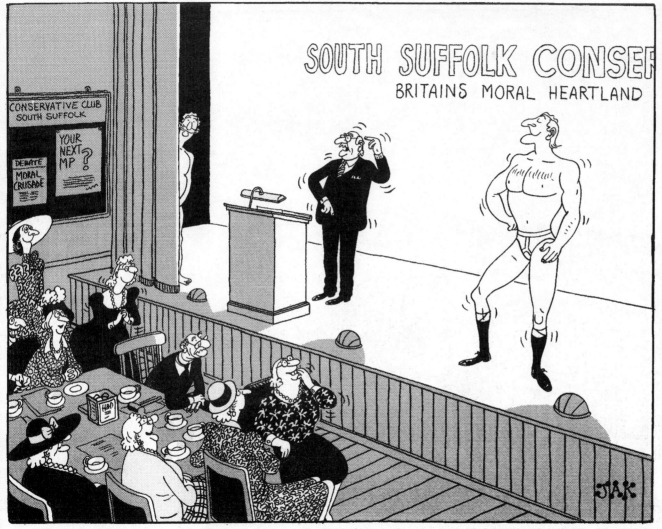

**Wednesday
12 January 1994**

Tory officials in Tim Yeo's South Suffolk constituency expressed dismay at his revelation that he fathered a baby when he was a student at Cambridge University. A Tory Party member who was at the secret meeting over the weekend said: "It has been made clear to him we no longer want him as our MP. When Mr Yeo attended the constituency party meeting only 24 hours before he resigned as a minister, he was asked if there were any other skeletons in his cupboard. He forgot to mention this second love child."

". . . next we have a made-to-order Tory MP – nothing up here and nothing down there!"

Thursday 13 January 1994

Battle lines were drawn in the Channel crossing war. It was revealed that Chunnel trains would whisk motorists between England and France for about the same price as ferries, but in under half the time. The announcement signalled a ferocious advertising war; the ferry companies emphasised the benefits of restaurants, shops and leisure facilities, while Chunnel operators pointed to speed and reliability.

"It's the in-flight entertainment!"

**Friday
14 January 1994**

EastEnders star Gillian Taylforth climbed into a Range Rover – to show a court how she did not perform a sex act with her boyfriend. Gillian fastened her seatbelt in the High Court car park and lowered her head over fiancé Geoff Knights's stomach in an attempt to prove the sex act would be impossible with her belt on. She eventually lost her libel action against The Sun newspaper.

"Fantastic! What else can you do in it?"

A private celebration for civil servants and chosen political journalists to say farewell to Gus O'Donnell, the Prime Minister's chief Press secretary, degenerated into a public row putting relations between Number 10 and the Press at an all-time low. A "leak" of a purported conversation at the leaving party, in which the Prime Minister threatened he would "f****** crucify" Cabinet Right-wingers for trouble-making over the Back to Basics policy, exploded 24 hours later when it appeared on the front page of The Sun and in the Daily Mail. Downing Street reacted furiously to what it claimed was "a malicious fiction".

"Our Prime Minister doesn't understand us!"

In one of the most explosive confrontations between the Prime Minister and Press, John Major's office issued categorical denials that he made threats against Thatcherite Ministers at a private party. Yet within hours of the party ending, reports were beginning to circulate of a bullish Prime Minister in robust and vindictive mood, ready to take on his party enemies.

"Oh! The usual Norma, and what sort of day did you have?"

Westminster remained gripped by speculation over what was, or was not, said by the Prime Minister at Gus O'Donnell's leaving do. And the position of Michael Brunson, ITN's fast-talking political editor, became ever more embarrassing. As the new chairman of the lobby, Brunson's job was to smooth relations between No 10 and the political press corps. Yet wild and unsubstantiated allegations continued to circulate.

". . . This is Michael Brunson, ITN, in a Tory interrogation dungeon somewhere in Whitehall!"

"Didn't you pay the service charge, Henry?"

Tory MP Michael Fabricant introduced a Bill which would stamp out the practice of paying hefty fixed service charges on top of the price of a restaurant meal, leaving the customer to determine whether a tip was justified. Apart from Greece, Britain is the only country in the EU to allow a compulsory service charge.

**Friday
21 January 1994**

The Football Association would not confirm Terry Venables as England's next football manager until the full extent of his involvement in Tottenham's financial dealings was disclosed. It would be more than three weeks before the FA Premier League inquiry into charges of irregularities at White Hart Lane was concluded and Venables appointed.

"They won't be much longer Mr Venables, they're just reminiscing about the old days!"

**Monday
24 January 1994**

Tim Yeo, the former environment minister, and Julia Stent, the mother of his baby daughter, were pictured leaving Langan's Brasserie in Mayfair after a three-hour lunch. Mr Yeo had said that he would keep in close contact with Miss Stent but friends were said to be worried at his apparent lack of tact in taking her to such a prominent restaurant on the day an interview with his wife, pledging support for him, appeared in The Times.

"It's a little discreet spot recommended by a fellow Tory MP!"

The Prince of Wales, heir to the throne of Australia, arrived in Sydney to begin a testing 12-day tour. Without the Princess of Wales, he had lost a potent crowd-puller whose presence guaranteed large and enthusiastic gatherings during their last visit, to Australia's Bicentennial celebrations in 1988.

"We thought it would generate more interest if we took Camilla along as well!"

EastEnders star Gillian Taylforth burst into tears as she faced another night of agony over her libel battle. She sobbed in the arms of fiancé Geoff Knights when the jury failed to reach a verdict on The Sun story claiming they performed a sex act in a car on an A1 slip-road. A huge cast of lawyers also awaited the outcome.

"It's been such a success, they're thinking of taking it up west!"

British and French
travellers awaited news
of an opening date for the
Channel tunnel.

"As a quarter of the journey will be in a tunnel, we'd like to show them what they're missing
of the Kent countryside!"

A budgerigar called Peter became the first suspected bird victim of passive smoking. Owner Eileen Wilson, 81, has smoked 40 a day for 64 years, and her habit proved too much for her six-year-old pet, who apparently developed lung cancer.

"Your dog doesn't look too good either!"

A report by the Public Accounts Committee, the body responsible for looking into the way taxpayers' money is spent, proved a crushing indictment of the way the modern British civil service works. It lifted the lid on a story of incompetence, improper conduct and fraud.

"No knighthood after running the department for 30 years?
I'm surprised you're not doing at least 10 years!"

Resentment that had been simmering in Britain's finest kitchens for years boiled over with the publication of the 1994 Michelin Guide. Several of the country's best-known chefs accused the celebrated guide of culinary chauvinism that ignored some of the best of British cooking. Britain has two three-star restaurants while France has 19.

"Well I didn't know he hadn't got his third star in the Michelin Guide!"

"Your usual table, Mr Lamont?"

**Tuesday
1 February 1994**

Battered Premier John Major was branded "weak and hopeless" in a devastating attack by the former Chancellor Norman Lamont. Times writer Ginny Dougary interviewed Lamont over lunch at Princess Diana's favourite restaurant, San Lorenzo, where he ripped Mr Major's character to shreds. Much of the subsequent debate centred on whether his comments had been on or off the record.

Wednesday 2 February 1994

The dramatic revamp of Radio 1 cost the station 1.4 million listeners, it was revealed. The shake-up, which led to the angry departure of veteran presenters Simon Bates and Dave Lee Travis, was supposed to attract a younger, trendier audience. But figures showed that listeners had deserted the BBC pop flagship in droves for commercial rivals.

"Well, you seem to be the only listener left, Mum! Mum . . ? Mum . . .?"

**Friday
4 February 1994**

President Clinton made a late effort to undermine the impact made by Gerry Adams' 48-hour visit to America. Mr Clinton tried to rescue the American relationship with Britain from the wreckage left by the Adams propaganda triumph. On both sides of the Atlantic, frantic damage-limitation attempts were under way.

**Monday
7 February 1994**

American parachutist Jim Miller landed on the roof of Buckingham Palace. He was lucky the Queen was not in residence or he would have been shot down before he could land, Scotland Yard sources said. Dozens of armed officers pounced on 30-year-old Miller, whose motorised parachute flight had been monitored by police for several miles. Before he was overpowered, the birdman stripped naked and smeared himself with green paint.

In a Gallup poll most voters – including many Tories – said they believed Labour leader John Smith was caring (81 per cent), competent (76), likable (74), and decisive (68). Of all voters, 33 per cent said they would be delighted if he formed a Labour Government, with 21 per cent dismayed and 45 per cent who would not mind. He sadly died before their confidence in him could be put to the test.

"If Labour gets in, would you be (a) frightened (b) horrified (c) terrified?"

European foreign ministers edged towards military intervention in Bosnia-Herzegovina when they backed the use of air power to try to break the siege of Sarajevo. The move came after John Major had called for "immediate, effective and more muscular action" to end the bombardment of the city.

"That was a near one!"

The world of postal history was shaken when one of the country's leading stamp and envelope dealers was fined £3,000 by Macclesfield magistrates after wrongly claiming that the signatures on two envelopes it sold were by Admiral Lord Nelson. David Shannon of Hertford, membership secretary of the Nelson Society, paid £250 for what he thought were letters signed by the naval hero. He later discovered the signatures were not only written by a right-handed man (Nelson lost his right arm in 1797) but were dated four years after he died in 1805.

"That's funny, Admiral Nelson, it looks nothing like your usual signature!"

John Major led a desperate attempt by the Tory high command to limit the political fallout from the death of Stephen Milligan, MP for Eastleigh. Milligan was found dead on the kitchen floor of his west London home. He was naked apart from a pair of stockings and a suspender belt, and had a cord around his neck.

"You've got a lot of ground to make up around here, PM. Look, there's another window with a Vote Labour poster!"

A married Tory MP was exposed as a love-cheat. Methodist lay preacher Hartley Booth, 47, who took over Margaret Thatcher's seat at the last election, confessed to a passionate, four-month affair with a former nude model. The revelation further damaged John Major's Back to Basics campaign – already reeling from a string of sex scandals.

"Not much in the news these days, is there, Mabel?"

The Sinn Fein president Gerry Adams gave another significant rebuff to the Anglo-Irish peace initiative when he urged Britain to persuade Northern Ireland's one million Protestants to back a united Ireland. Adams's demand was one already rejected by John Major, reinforcing the impression that he was preparing the ground for ditching the initiative. TV companies were still forced to broadcast an actor's voice to speak the words of any Sinn Fein or IRA member.

"Tonight, John Major speaks to the people of the Irish Republic.
His voice will be dubbed by Arthur Mullard!"

**Wednesday
16 February 1994**

The aftermath of recent
Tory sex scandals
rumbled on in the Press.

"Why don't we hear anything about Labour MPs? Are they all doctored when they join?"

Thursday 17 February 1994

The Government revealed that prescription charges were to rise 50p to £4.75 from 1 April, an increase six times the rate of inflation. The 11.8 per cent rise was immediately condemned by Labour as an "outrageous tax on the sick".

"The prescription charge finished him off!"

The campaign to legalise euthanasia was set back by a report from peers that rejected the practice because of fears for the old and disabled. The unanimous report, from the House of Lords' committee on medical ethics, was an unexpected blow for organisations that want to bring Britain into line with The Netherlands, where euthanasia is practised.

"Wake up, m'lud, the euthanasia man is doing his rounds!"

The string of Tory scandals, culminating in the resignation of Hartley Booth, the Finchley MP who confessed to a close friendship with his former researcher, turned John Major's back to basics campaign into something of a joke.

COMMONS BAR

"Did I hear the division bell?"

Dennis Skinner, the hard-Left scourge of Conservative policies and peccadilloes for 24 years, displayed uncharacteristic reserve after lurid reports about his private life. The 62-year-old Labour MP was said to have had a secret relationship with his Commons researcher, Lois Blasenheim, 47.

"Evening, Mr Skinner! Nice night for it!"

MPs voted by a massive majority to lower the age of consent for homosexual males from 21 to 18. Voting was 427 to 162. A proposal to reduce the age to 16, in line with the age of consent for heterosexual sex, was rejected by 307 votes to 280.

PAUL CALLAN HOUSE ❯

ETON COLLEGE
EST 1440

"I don't care what Parliament decided on Monday night, Watson.
A little black number would be more suitable for this school!"

**Friday
25 February 1994**

Profits at National Westminster Bank enjoyed a 169 per cent lift, to £989 million. NatWest also announced that it planned 4,200 job cuts in 1994. Staff numbers fell by 17,500 from their peak of 109,000 in 1989, said the bank. More than 3,800 jobs were axed and 130 branches were closed in 1993.

"Fantastic redundancy figures, Wilkins. There's only you and me left – and you're fired!"

"If we get the contracts back, how much 'bung' do you expect?"

A crisis between Britain and Malaysia loomed in the wake of the row over the Pergau Dam project. In a backlash against allegations of corruption, the Malaysian government looked certain to announce a halt to trade contracts with Britain. Mr Major sent an 11th-hour message to Malaysian leader Dr Mahathir Mohamed, urging second thoughts about any embargo.

**Tuesday
1 March 1994**

Scotland Yard planned an unprecedented Royal Crimewatch TV appeal – to try to recover priceless heirlooms and personal jewellery stolen from Prince Charles in a burglary at St James's Palace. Millions of viewers hoped for a glimpse of the famous gold cufflinks engraved with intertwined Cs – said to have been given to the Prince by Camilla Parker Bowles on the eve of his wedding. But royal insiders claimed they never existed.

". . .but the good news is – we've found your cuff links!"

Wednesday 2 March 1994

The Archbishop of Canterbury was furious with John Gummer over the Environment Secretary's conversion to Roman Catholicism. Gummer, a prominent Anglican layman, crossed to Rome at a secret ceremony in a tiny church in Westminster. Gummer infuriated Dr George Carey by claiming the Church of England's decision to allow women priests meant it had become little more than a "sect".

"Just a confession, Mr Gummer, not a party political broadcast!"

**Thursday
3 March 1994**

Romeo Major James Hewitt was accused by a Sunday newspaper of betraying Princess Diana. The People revealed that the upper-crust charmer used the Princess for his own schemes to make money and tried to hawk the cruellest lie of all – that he had made love to Diana. The 35-year-old Life Guards officer raked in around £100,000 from the sale of his account of their friendship. Princess Diana was reported to be dismayed at how far Hewitt was prepared to go to cash in.

". . . and when you've done the right thing, Hewitt, I trust you'll leave your royalties to the regiment!"

The press continued to debate John Gummer's conversion to the Roman Catholic Church. The Environment Secretary was outspoken against women priests and condemned the Church of England as a sect. His move was seen as likely to encourage more waverers opposing the ordination of women to take the road to Rome.

ST GEORGE'S ANGLICAN CHURCH

JAK

"John Gummer's doing very well, considering he's only been in a week!"

"It's viewing by appointment only!"

**Tuesday
8 March 1994**

Twenty years after Richard Nixon left Washington in disgrace, the ghosts of Watergate gathered around the White House. The long-simmering scandal about the financial dealings of Bill and Hillary Clinton in Arkansas came to a boil and once more the American presidency was in crisis. To escape accusations of using improper influence to blunt investigation of the Whitewater affair, the president fired his chief legal adviser, Bernard Nussbaum, and claimed he had no knowledge of Mr Nussbaum's dubious efforts on his behalf.

The scale of the Prince of Wales's loss after a burglary from St James's Palace emerged as he took the unprecedented step of allowing photographs of his personal possessions to be issued in the hope of having some returned. Cuff links, sleeve links, pens and tie, stock and stick pins were taken in the burglary. Encrusted with rubies, emeralds and diamonds, and by names such as Fabergé and Annabel Jones, the items had a market value of around £65,000.

"Nice silver cigarette case, Fingers! Nice Fabergé cuff links!
You haven't got a gold engraved Hunter to tell me the time, have you?"

**Friday
11 March 1994**

Terrorists came within feet of causing carnage at Heathrow Airport when they fired five home-made mortars at a main runway from a car. The mortars failed to detonate, but two missiles lay on the tarmac for 40 minutes while 24 planes took off. Police received a bomb warning, but were at first unaware why 10 cars were ablaze outside the Excelsior Hotel. The terrorists' car and other vehicles caught fire when the shells were launched.

"That was a truly remarkable experience, Miss Jenkins. Now, where did I leave the office car?"

"Und I got this one for eating British beef!"

The Germans planned a ban on imports of beef from Britain arguing that because BSE – the so-called mad cow disease – had been found in the meat, it could pose a threat to humans. Specialists at the Ministry of Agriculture, Fisheries and Food claimed the risk was "remote".

"I'm afraid we'll have to take the company plane back, Sir Peter!"

**Monday
14 March 1994**

The Government was rocked by allegations that Chief of Defence Staff Sir Peter Harding had conducted a passionate affair with the beautiful ex-wife of former senior Tory MP Sir Antony Buck. Sir Peter was accused of having a "very intimate relationship" with Sir Antony's Spanish-born former wife Bienvenida Perez-Blanco while she was still married.

Tuesday 15 March 1994

The chief of Britain's armed forces, Sir Peter Harding, quit over his affair with the Spanish wife of an ex-Tory defence minister. And furious MPs demanded an inquiry into the security risks of Sir Peter's two-year fling. He wrote passionate letters to his mistress and was later photographed kissing her in the street, which made him a prime target for blackmail.

"We're doing a Mori poll. Is your mistress Spanish, Swedish or Welsh?"

Drunken sailor David Quilter was hauled in front of a court martial because he bit a woman naval officer on the bottom in a Greek harbour bar. Quilter, a 27-year-old Petty Officer on the aircraft carrier *Invincible*, admitted assault and bodily harm charges.

"He didn't stop at the bum, sir!"

Thursday 17 March 1994

The ethics and dangers of choosing babies by gender became the centre of a fierce controversy. It was sparked by the story of Gillian and Neil Clark, who paid £650 for the treatment that added little Sophie May to their two sons. MPs, religious leaders and doctors warned that the practice could cause irreparable damage to society by producing a population overloaded with boys.

"As a matter of fact you were a designer baby. Why, what seems to be the problem, Roger?"

Child-minders who want the right to smack naughty children with their parents' agreement were handed a victory in the High Court. A judge came down on the side of 34-year-old Mrs Anne Davis, who was banned as a paid child-minder when she refused to sign an undertaking not to use corporal punishment. Supporters of smacking hailed Mr Justice Wilson's decision as a triumph for common sense and family values.

"And give him a good thrashing every half-hour or he'll take advantage of you!"

**Sunday
20 March 1994**

The mortar attacks on
Heathrow airport
prompted a massive
security response.

"Do you want a collision damage waiver?"

**Monday
21 March 1994**

A top-level investigation into how £1 million of State money was spent refurbishing official homes of senior RAF officers was launched. The inquiry was ordered by Defence Secretary Malcolm Rifkind following revelations about the use of public funds on the houses.

"Bye darling, have a nice day at the office!"

"Apparently he goes down very well with the Croats!"

Twenty thousand soccer fans gave a roar of appreciation to the band of the Coldstream Guards on a football pitch in besieged Sarajevo. The 38-strong band flew from RAF Lyneham, in Wiltshire, at the request of UN forces commander in Bosnia Lieutenant-General Sir Michael Rose, who felt their half-time entertainment would be the perfect morale-booster for civilians and troops alike.

Wednesday 23 March 1994

Baroness Thatcher fainted as she addressed hundreds of Chilean businessmen. She had been speaking for 30 minutes when she fell forward at the lectern hitting her face against a microphone. Her husband Sir Denis rushed to support her and helped her to a seat. She had been suffering from an intestinal infection for 24 hours but insisted on delivering the speech.

"It was a different chef, Lady Thatcher!"

John Major announced an invitation to veterans of the Third Reich to march through London, 50 years after the end of World War II. The servicemen, both serving and retired, were expected to be allowed to wear uniforms and campaign medals in the joint parade. But Tory MPs accused him of insensitivity to the British people who suffered the loss of loved ones.

"I captured that one on D-Day!"

**Friday
25 March 1994**

Education Secretary John Patten ordered an inquiry into claims that primary school pupils were taught about oral sex. Nurse Sue Brady was accused of explaining intimate sex details to 10- and 11-year-olds at Highfield Primary school, near Leeds. Pupils were said to have acted out the roles of "mummy", "daddy" and "mummy's lover" during the lesson.

"If you want to know what I'm doing with Nurse, Headmaster, could you stand over with the rest of the class!"

Disney magic came to the Tower of London when the Queen opened the new home for the Crown Jewels with a fanfare of regal music, fibre-optic lighting, video screens and plastic souvenirs. Tower bosses got their inspiration for the £10 million jewel house during a visit to Disney World in Florida.

"You take it right back, Darren, and tell the Queen you're sorry!"

A team of Army climbers were snatched from a treacherous gully called the Place of Death after three weeks in a cave on Mount Kinabalu in Borneo. A helicopter spotted the letters SOS picked out in white pebbles against the black backdrop of the mountain. They were not the only people in need of rescue.

"We'll all sit tight here, something's bound to turn up to save us!"

Tuesday 29 March 1994

Sir Patrick Mayhew, the Northern Ireland Secretary, supported a decision to grant Gerry Adams, the Sinn Fein president, legal aid to fight the Government ban on him entering mainland Britain. He said the decision showed that the British system of justice was "fair, equal and unpartisan".

"Ah, Mr Adams. Would you like to select one of these lawyers to represent you in your forthcoming action!"

**Wednesday
30 March 1994**

Silvio Berlusconi, the
media tycoon, began
negotiations to form a
Right-wing government
after his Freedom
Alliance won 366 of the
630 Chamber of Deputies
seats and a landslide
victory in the Italian
election.

"Go on, Richard, Berlusconi only started his party three months ago!"

England's cricketers collapsed to a humiliating 40 runs for eight wickets overnight in the West Indies as they chased 194 runs to win the Third Test. They failed, the last two wickets adding just six more runs in the morning.

"There didn't seem much point in carrying on!"

To clamp down on a national epidemic of skin cancer, it was announced the BBC and ITV weather reports would carry sunburn warnings. Sunbathers would be told whether the risk was low, medium, high or very high, and the average time it would take certain skin types to burn.

"We interrupt the weather to broadcast an urgent sunburn warning!"

D-Day veterans planning a 50th anniversary reunion in France lost out on their hotels to make room for American film crews, it was revealed. The 100 old soldiers were first told their rooms had been commandeered for an official party of VIPs. But later it emerged the veterans had lost their places to the US television networks. The French subsequently backed down.

"Get those medals off, Henri. We don't want people to think we let old soldiers in this hotel!"

Wednesday 6 April 1994

Former Tory Minister Sir Nicholas Fairbairn made an astonishing attack on John Major. He branded the Prime Minister "a ventriloquist's dummy" and "a softie" and insisted he should stand down because his "benevolent and inadequate" leadership was tearing the Conservative Party apart.

"The trouble with John Major is that he just doesn't understand ordinary people!"

England's cricket selectors had their most important Caribbean assignment – to pick a team capable of halting the West Indian march towards a blackwash in Barbados.
Mike Atherton's team did, in fact, win.

"There didn't seem much point in getting changed any more!"

**Sunday
10 April 1994**

Amid howls of protest, the French government changed its mind about the despicable treatment of D-Day veterans who were to be booted out of their long-booked hotel.

"Waiter! This bloody menu's all in French!"

**Monday
11 April 1994**

After the previous year's fiasco the Grand National proved a good bet for comic Freddie Starr. His horse Minnehoma romped home as the 16-1 winner.

"Never mind what he looks like, see what he puts his bets on!"

**Wednesday
13 April 1994**

Extreme Russian nationalist Vladimir Zhirinovsky ripped plants from the ground to throw at demonstrators ranged against him as he visited the Council of Europe in Strasbourg. Then "Mad Vlad", who controls a quarter of the seats in the Moscow parliament, said Russia should hit back at Nato to help the "victims" of its policy, even at the risk of starting a major war.

"That's the interpreter explaining the finer points of Zhirinovsky's speech!"

A worldwide hunt was launched to find a new 007, following Timothy Dalton's surprise announcement that he was quitting the role he first played in 1987.

SEARCH FOR NEW 007

JAK

"Well, Pussy Galore didn't wear a vest, Vera!"

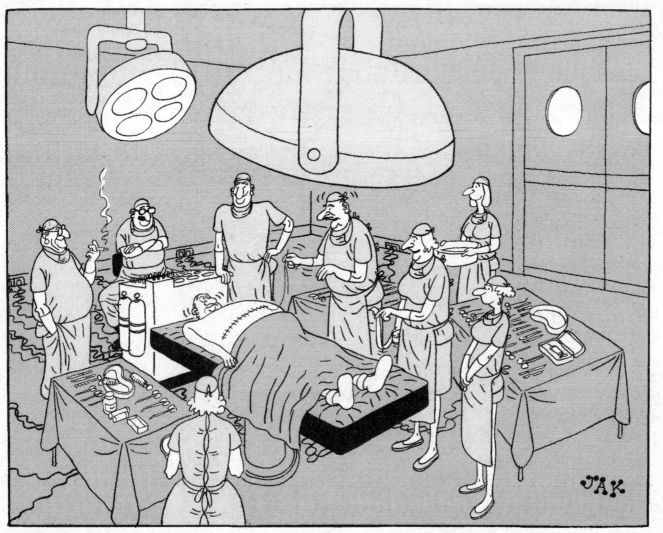

**Thursday
15 April 1994**

Health Secretary
Virginia Bottomley came
under renewed fire as it
transpired that two
pensioners had been
turned away from
hospitals because of their
age which made them
unsuitable cases for
treatment under the
NHS's free-market ethos.

"I'm afraid you'll have to take the stitches out yourself in a few days' time as you'll be over 65 by then!"

**Sunday
17 April 1994**

Amateur golfer Fred Buckingham began a unique libel action against two members of his club after they accused him of cheating by dropping a new ball out of his pocket when his original was lost. Notttingham court heard that retired businessman Mr Buckingham's life revolved around the game.

"Never mind a caddie, if you're playing here I'd take a good lawyer around with you!"

D-Day veterans throughout Britain pondered over ways of celebrating the forthcoming anniversary. Brewers poured cold water on a Government suggestion that beer prices should be cut on 6 June to the D-Day level of 1s 1d a pint (about 5p). An independent brewer said: "We might be persuaded if the Government reduced excise duty to 1944 levels first."

". . .Vera Lynn singing 'There'll be blue birds over the white cliffs of Dover' or a D-Day kissogram girl?"

After months of
dithering, the United
Nations got tough with
the Serbs. British
warplanes went into
action attacking Serbian
tanks. The planes were
defending the town
of Gorazde – a
UN-designated safe
haven – which had
become the latest target
for the Serbs' ethnic
cleansing.

Thursday 21 April 1994

Coronation Street emerged the easy winner in its first Monday viewing clash with EastEnders. Viewing figures showed 15 million soap fans watched ITV's double helping of The Street, while eight million tuned into the BBC.

"Bloody snobs!"

**Friday
22 April 1994**

The British Legion demanded that John Major scrap his "tasteless" jamboree to celebrate the 50th anniversary of the D-Day landings. The Prime Minister planned a party in Hyde Park, with forces sweetheart Dame Vera Lynn as star guest. But furious old soldiers said the junket would cheapen the loss of 40,000 British troops in France. Dame Vera eventually agreed. Meanwhile, UN plans to settle the Bosnian crisis foundered.

"Of course, we'll have to get it approved by Vera Lynn!"

**Sunday
24 April 1994**

War veterans called for the showpiece event of Britain's D-Day anniversary celebrations to be scrapped. In the most serious challenge yet to the programme of commemoration, which was condemned as "frivolous", the Royal British Legion demanded the cancellation of a massive jamboree in Hyde Park. Meanwhile, other veterans had their own plans.

"I hope you've done enough fritters, Mabel, there's a queue right around the block!"

Germany threatened to unilaterally ban British beef imports over "mad cow disease" fears. Bonn sought EU support for a ban, citing fears that meat from cattle infected with the fatal brain disease BSE could endanger human health.

"Offhand, I'd say it was the British beef!"

As John Major promised new help for the disabled, hospital cutbacks began to bite.

"Usually the long walk finishes them off!"

**Thursday
12 May 1994
(last edition)**

Victoria Scott struggled with conflicting loyalties as she advised her Government minister father to quit. The 28-year-old lobbyist for the disabled had been closely involved in promoting the Civil Rights Bill which Nicholas Scott helped to destroy when the Bill was "talked out" by 80 hostile amendments.

"Hi, dad! Can I borrow the car tonight!"

**Friday
13 May 1994**

Coca-Cola saw its sales plummet by almost half – from 63 to 33 per cent – in Sainsbury's branches after the own-label Classic Cola drink appeared. But manufacturing giant Coca-Cola's claim that it was a "copycat" product forced Sainsbury to think again.

"Number 20173 looks the least like a Coca-Cola can, sir, but we do have a problem with stacking!"

**Sunday
15 May 1994**

Jordans village cricket club won a historic victory when a judge ruled that it could play again on the village green it had used for 60 years. Design engineer David Lacey and his wife Rosa-Maria were left with a £20,000 bill for taking on the club and demanding it was barred from the green unless 25ft-high nets were put up to stop cricket balls hitting their house.

"He was just describing the amenities when he was struck by a beautifully flighted six!"

**Monday
16 May 1994**

Thieves pulled off one of Britain's biggest house burglaries, taking treasure worth millions of pounds from a leading private art collection. Burglars broke into Luton Hoo, a Georgian mansion set in 4,000 acres of Capability Brown parkland two miles south of Luton, through a ground-floor window. Fabergé eggs, ornaments and jewellery were among the haul.

"I'm afraid we'll have to eat with our fingers – the thieves got simply everything over the weekend!"

Tuesday
17 May 1994

An Austrian hotel boss ordered stunned holidaymakers to bed as the clock struck nine. The guests did not believe the hotelier was serious – until one of the party was clipped around the ear for not obeying his orders. Then Herr Wagner, manager of the three-star Hotel Kaiserblick in Soll near Innsbruck, began ranting and raving at how British tourists were always drinking supermarket beer and gin and keeping other guests awake until the early hours. The guests were mostly elderly folk looking for a quiet rest, but Herr Wagner maintained: "This is my hotel and they will do as I say."

"They're making the Austrians go to bed at nine in retaliation!"

Wednesday 18 May 1994

It was announced that handguns would be openly worn by police in London for the first time. They would only be carried by specially-trained Metropolitan officers on patrol in the capital 24 hours a day in 12 armed response vehicles instead of the previous five. The officers would be allowed to wear their Smith & Wesson .38 pistols on their belts at all times, carry 18 rounds of ammunition in pouches and draw weapons without authority from a high-ranking officer.

"Go ahead, punk! Make my day!"

Princess Diana helped save the life of a tramp drowning in a canal near Regent's Park when she ordered her chauffeur to dial 999 on her mobile phone while she pulled Martin O'Donoghue from the water. Diana helped turn the 42-year-old vagrant on his side and watched as he was given the kiss of life

"I was just going down for the third time, when this vision of loveliness saved me –
I think I'll jump in again tomorrow!"

Monday 23 May 1993

A blooming great row came to a head on the day of the opening of the Chelsea Flower Show over flowers grown by exhibitors and those bought by the truckload from wholesalers. John Metcalf and Joe Ambridge both had breathtaking stands in the Great Marquee at the show but John grew all his exhibits while Joe had never seen any of the £1,900 worth of lilies on his stall until they were delivered ready cut and carefully packed in boxes. The judges were not allowed to make any distinction between blooms painstakingly nurtured by experts and those simply bought in from industrial-scale growers.

"What have you got for a fiver that I can exhibit at the Chelsea Flower Show?"

**Tuesday
24 May 1994**

A BBC decision to give gay staff paid honeymoon leave and £75 "wedding gift" vouchers outraged MPs. Tory Harry Greenway said: "This is a serious abuse of public money." He urged National Heritage Secretary Peter Brooke to slash licence fees unless the idea was dropped.

"I'm sure you'd like to know your licence fee was well spent –
Kevin and Wayne had a simply fabulous honeymoon!"

Wednesday 25 May 1994

The fierce row over claims of dirty work in the flower beds continued at the Chelsea Flower Show. The diehards, led by John Metcalf, insisted that all the blooms should have been planted and grown by their exhibitors and poured scorn on those who imported boxes by the truckload to impress judges.

"Fascinating! Did you grow it yourself!"

**Friday
27 May 1994**

A furious Richard Branson hit out after losing his bid to run the new national lottery. He condemned the decision to award it to a profit-making consortium as "perhaps the most crass" made by any government. The Camelot Group fought off seven rival bidders, including the wealthy Virgin boss, to win the coveted licence. Rival airline boss Lord King may not have been so upset at the decision.

"Lord King has been inconsolable since Richard Branson lost the lottery contract!"

The sexual boasts of former Defence Minister Alan Clark rebounded on him, wrecking his hopes of reviving his political career. Top Tories were dismayed by the revelation that he seduced a judge's wife and her two young daughters. Mrs Valerie Harkess, who did not know that the girls had been involved with Mr Clark until long after it happened, described the 66-year-old multi-millionaire as "a depraved animal".

"I was just entertaining this gal, when her enraged mother charged me. Luckily, I bagged both of them!"

The tale of the Minister, the judge, his wife, her daughter and their sex lives grabbed all the headlines as Judge James Harkess, 64, and two of the women once infamously bedded by former minister Alan Clark – his wife Valerie 57, and stepdaughter Josephine, 34 – boarded a plane in Cape Town to fly to Britain.

"The sex-drive of a stoat, the morals of a Tunisian brothel-keeper – gentlemen,
I think our search for a new Tory leader is over!"

**Friday
3 June 1994**

D-Day veterans arrived in Normandy for the 50th anniversary of the landings.

"If you'd been watching, General, I did have it with me on D-Day!"

**Monday
6 June 1944**

As the D-Day veterans returned to the Normandy beaches a warm welcome awaited most of them.

"Are you sure you'll recognise him after all these years, maman?"

D-Day veterans came back from the celebrations in Normandy, some with trophies.

"This is Fritz! We captured him three miles from the beachhead!"

West Indian Brian Lara made cricket history when he became the first batsman to break the 500 barrier. Playing for Warwickshire against Durham, he set cricket's highest individual score of 501 not out. This beat the 499 set by Hanif Mohammed 35 years earlier.

"Exactly how long were you bowling at Edgbaston?"

"Cholmondeley-Warner! I'd warned you about telling those Irish jokes – now you're up before the CRE!"

A storm erupted over a £6,000 compensation award to an Irishman tormented by jokes at work. Machinist Trevor McAuley, 36, told an industrial tribunal that the daily abuse ruined his work and affected his family life. He did not mind Irish jokes but drew the line at being called a "typical thick Paddy". He won his claim of racial discrimination against his former employers, Auto Alloys Foundry, of Blackwell, Derbyshire.